AF259342

The 30-Day Voice Athlete Strategy
A Daily Guide with Secret Sauce to Move Beyond Obstacles
Keaver Brenai

Edited by KJ Jones
Book and cover design by Michael Campbell,
    MC Writing Services

ISBN: 978-1-62660-191-8

THE 30-DAY VOICE ATHLETE STRATEGY

A Daily Guide with Secret Sauce
to Move Beyond Obstacles

KEAVER BRENAI

IV

FOREWORD

The performance world has changed. Public speakers, podcasters, voiceover artists, and stage and screen actors now work in an industry that moves faster, demands more, and expects consistency at a level few could have imagined a decade ago. Technology has expanded opportunity, and increased pressure. Sessions run longer. Deadlines are tighter. Competition is global.

In this climate, endurance matters as much as ability. The performers who build lasting careers aren't only gifted, they prepare intentionally. They understand the voice is not separate from the body or the mind, and they train, protect their energy, and care for their instrument the way an athlete cares for their body.

The 30-Day Voice Athlete Strategy: A Daily Guide with Secret Sauce for Moving Beyond Obstacles speaks directly to this reality with a practical reframe: voice professionals are athletes of sound. Sustained performance depends on conditioning, recovery, and daily habits that support long-term strength. Success isn't built on bursts of effort, but on steady preparation.

What makes this book especially valuable is its usability. Instead of abstract motivation, it offers clear tools you can apply immediately: care checklists, warm-up and recovery routines, mindset strategies, and performance practices that are designed for real-world demands—from remote sessions to high-stakes auditions. These aren't theories, they're habits that produce results.

Most importantly, this work reinforces a truth often overlooked in creative industries, longevity is planned. Sustainable careers are built through discipline, consistency, and respect for the voice that makes the work possible.

Whether you're just beginning or deep into your professional journey, this book is an empowering roadmap, not only for performing better today, but for building the strength, resilience, and confidence to perform for years to come.

This book is for educational purposes and is not a substitute for medical advice. If you experience persistent vocal pain or hoarseness, consult an ENT specialist or a qualified healthcare professional.

PREFACE

This book is for voice professionals who love their work and want to do it with strength, clarity, and confidence for years to come.

It emerged from a familiar pattern in performance-driven industries: highly capable people pushing beyond healthy limits, equating overwork with dedication, and realizing too late that talent alone cannot sustain a career. The voice is expressive and resilient, but it is also vulnerable when care, rest, and preparation are neglected.

The 30-Day Voice Athlete Strategy: A Daily Guide with Secret Sauce for Moving Beyond Obstacles challenges that cycle with a more sustainable question: How do I prepare for a lifetime of speaking and performance? That shift changes the entire approach. Rest becomes strategy. Care becomes discipline. Mindset becomes a skill you can train.

The pages that follow are designed to be practical and realistic. You'll find daily tools and simple routines to support high-pressure performance while safeguarding health and energy. This is not a strict, one-size-fits-all program. It's a flexible framework you can adopt to your career, schedule, and season, strengthening not only your voice but the person behind it.

If these practices help you perform with greater confidence, recover with greater wisdom, and stay connected to the joy of using your voice, then it has done what it was written to do.

VIII

INTRODUCTION

Standing out in today's professional voice industry requires more than talent. Talent may open the door, but mental resilience, physical awareness, and disciplined care are what keep you in the room. As the industry becomes more technologically demanding, voice professionals are expected to perform at higher levels for longer hours, often under intense pressure, while protecting the one asset they cannot replace.

This is where the Voice Athlete Method begins.

Elite athletes don't rely on natural ability alone. They condition the body, train the mind, and treat recovery as part of performance. When voice professionals adopt that same mindset, consistency replaces burnout, confidence replaces anxiety, and longevity becomes deliberate.

Your voice works through your body. Breath, posture, hydration, sleep, nutrition, emotional regulation, and focus all shape how you sound and how you show up. Ignoring these factors doesn't make them less important, it makes performance less reliable. The Voice Athlete understands that caring for the body is not an indulgence, it's professionalism.

This book isn't about quick wins or pushing to exhaustion. It's a sustainable, high-performance approach that respects both the craft and the calling. Inside, you'll learn how to train your mindset for focus and endurance, protect vocal health with daily habits, and prepare effectively for 'game day' in auditions, recording sessions, public speaking, teaching, theatre, film, or podcasting.

You'll also learn when to push and when to rest, how to recognize early warning signs, and why recovery is not a luxury but a competitive advantage. In voice-driven careers, success isn't defined by your best day, it's defined by how consistently you can deliver across many seasons.

The Voice Athlete Method isn't about doing more. It's about training smarter, caring more deeply, and performing intentionally. Welcome to an approach that honors your voice, your body, and your mindset as a championship team.

HOW TO USE THE VOICE ATHLETE METHOD

The 30-Day Voice Athlete Strategy is a structured daily training cycle built on the Voice Athlete Method, a framework for vocal stamina, mental resilience, and long-term performance. Like an athletic program, each day builds on the last. The "secret sauce" is the consistent blend of preparation, recovery, mindset, and daily care that strengthens awareness, discipline, and sustainable performance across mind, body, and voice.

Every day includes both training and a RESToday moment. Progress comes through rhythm, not intensity.

This program does not ask for perfection. It asks for intention. Lasting change begins with awareness.

To deepen the work, consider pairing each day with 10-20 minutes of meditation or mindful stillness. Regulating the nervous system enhances focus, steadies breath, and supports vocal consistency. When practiced before or after your daily training, consistency matters more than timing. For additional guided recovery and focus practices, explore meditations at RESTodayApp.com.

Before moving forward, pause.

Take a few minutes to reflect honestly on the question below. Write your answer without editing or overanalyzing.

What does becoming a Voice Athlete require of me, not only in skill, but in care, discipline, and mindset?

There are no right answers. This is not about comparison. It is about clarity.

Use the prompts below to reflect on a few more questions:

1. Do I see myself reacting to demands, or preparing for them?
2. Which daily habits support my vocal health and focus? Which undermine them?
3. How does my body feel before, during, and after sessions?
4. Where do I push beyond sustainable limits?
5. Have I treated care and recovery as optional rather than essential?

Return to these questions whenever you feel rushed, disconnected, or uncertain. Awareness becomes choice. Choice becomes habit. Habit becomes identity.

When you begin to see yourself as a Voice Athlete, your standards shift. Warm-ups become non-negotiable. Recovery becomes strategic. Mindset becomes trained rather than hoped for.

You are not simply a performer responding to opportunity. You are a prepared professional building longevity. Every choice off the mic shows up on it. Lace up. Hydrate. Train wisely. Enjoy the reps. I see you!

DAY 1
FOCUS AND ENDURANCE

Strengthening the mindset to perform under
pressure while protecting the voice.

Every performance requires focus, but endurance decides if that focus can last. In professional voice performance, pressure seldom comes with warning. High-stakes auditions, long filming sessions, tight recording schedules, and last-minute script changes demand that you be prepared, not just talented. The Voice Athlete doesn't rely on adrenaline to push through. They train their mindset beforehand and protect their voice so it can perform again tomorrow.

Lock in: Name your #1 distraction today, then mute it.

Endurance isn't just a personality trait, it's a skill developed through preparation. Mental resilience enables you to stay present when the stakes increase, while physical care safeguards your voice from fatigue and strain. When mindset and body cooperate, performance becomes steady rather than reactive. You stop hoping for a 'good day.' Instead, you build reliability through consistent daily habits.

Today begins with awareness. Before you try to improve anything, you need to recognize how you handle pressure right now. This is where training starts, not by pushing yourself harder, but by paying close attention. Where is focus needed, and endurance necessary?

Train Today

- Where does pressure most impact my focus?
- How do urgency and stress affect how my voice feels or sounds?
- What would it look like to protect my voice before it feels strained?

RESToday Reflection

I intentionally train my mind and guard my voice. Write your thoughts.

____

____

____

____

____

____

DAY 2
TIME, TRAINING, AND RECOVERY

*The athlete's proactive approach to
time, training, and recovery.*

Professional athletes do not separate performance from preparation. What happens between competitions is just as important as what occurs on game day. The same applies to voice professionals. Your voice does not warm up instantly or recover automatically, it depends directly on how focused you manage your time, energy, and habits.

Vocal health is about prevention, not correction. Drinking water before speaking, warming up gently, respecting fatigue, and resting without guilt may seem small, but these daily habits protect the vocal folds, reduce inflammation, and support clarity and stamina over time. Their effects add up quietly. What you do regularly matters more than what you do occasionally.

Hydration check: Take 7 sips right now. (Yes, count.) Whisper, "I'm worth it."

The Voice Athlete views time differently. Instead of cramming preparation into tight spots, they make room for it. Recovery is an integral part of the process. When rest is scheduled with a purpose in mind, performance becomes more consistent and less stressful. Today, consider asking not how much you can push, but how effectively you can prepare.

Hydrate as if it's your job... because it is!

Train Today

- How do I currently organize my time around vocal work?
- Where do I rush instead of taking time to prepare?
- Which habits protect my voice? What weakens it?

RESToday Reflection

Pick one preventative habit to focus on this week.

____

____

____

____

____

____

____

DAY 3
STAMINA, MINDSET, AND PERFORMANCE ON GAME DAY

*Performing confidently, flexibly, and
with control under pressure.*

Peak performance is rarely about pushing harder in the moment, it's about how well you prepared long before the moment arrived. Stamina in voice work isn't just vocal endurance, it includes mental clarity, emotional regulation, and physical readiness working together. When any of these elements are neglected, performance becomes unpredictable.

Game-day energy: Record at 7am one day this week.

Your voice is your power. Like any voice, it responds best to proactive care. Proper hydration, rest, and mindful technique keep the voice reliable even during long sessions and stressful days. Waiting until fatigue shows up is already too late. The Voice Athlete trains before strain.

On the bench or in the game, confidence on game day comes from trust, not luck. When you trust your preparation, nerves soften. You adapt more easily. You stay present. Instead of forcing results, you allow your training to carry you. This is what separates survival from mastery.

Train Today

- What makes me feel confident on 'game day?'
- How do I respond when pressure rises?
- What habits could help me feel steadier and more prepared?

RESToday Reflection

Preparation helps confidence replace panic.

DAY 4
ARTICULATION CHALLENGE

*Enhancing clarity through coordination,
control, and intentional repetition.*

Clear articulation isn't about speed, it's about control.
For the Voice Athlete, precision comes from coordination,
awareness, and deliberate repetition. Every sound you
produce results from breath, tongue, jaw, lips, and resonance working together. When one area tenses or overuses
muscles, clarity declines.

Tongue twisters are not just novelty exercises; they are
athletic drills. When practiced slowly and with purpose,
they reveal where tension is hidden and how efficiency can
be achieved. They develop flexibility and responsiveness
similarly to how strength training builds muscle control.
The aim is not perfection, but ease.

**Tongue gym cross fit: Say
"Unique New York" x7, slow
and clean, then with speed.**

Today's practice encourages curiosity rather than judgment. Pay attention to how your voice feels. Where does
sound flow smoothly? Where does it tighten up? Precision improves when you listen carefully. Control isn't
forced, it develops naturally.

Train Today

Tongue Twisters Articulation Challenge

Read slowly, then read with intention.

- Healthy voices prioritize hydration, harmony, and consistent care.
- Smooth esophageal airflow eases every expressive effort.
- Flexible vocal folds move freely for precise finesse.
- The tongue works tirelessly to master smooth transitions.
- Teeth touch lightly to soften sharp consonants.
- Humidifiers assist in hydrating hardworking harmonics.
- Tea helps soothe tired throats thoughtfully.
- Balanced breathing fosters bold, buoyant delivery.
- Resonance radiates when relaxation prevails.
- Recovery routines restore a dependable range.

RESToday Reflection

Which sounds feel easy? Which sounds feel tense?

____

____

____

____

DAY 5
ARTICULATION ENDURANCE

*Creating clarity and control that endures
from the first take to the final.*

At the start of a session, clarity often comes easily. Your mouth is relaxed, your breath steady, and each consonant lands cleanly. Words feel effortless. But professional voice work rarely ends after the first few minutes. Sessions stretch longer than expected. Retakes pile up. Energy dips. Fatigue quietly sets in. And that is when technique, not talent, determines the outcome.

Articulation is athletic work. Every sound requires coordination among the tongue, lips, jaw, breath, and resonance. These small muscles move constantly, shaping language with precision and speed. Like any muscle group, they tire when overused or undertrained. When fatigue sets in, shortcuts appear. Consonants soften. Words blur together. The jaw tightens. The throat compensates. What starts as subtle tension can gradually turn into strain or inconsistency.

The Voice Athlete knows that endurance isn't built by rushing through practice. It develops through mindful repetition. Training beyond the 'easy' point teaches your muscles how to stay responsive even when energy is low. Just as a runner trains for the final mile, you prepare for the final mile, the moment when focus might slip. Endurance means your last read sounds as strong and connected as your first. That consistency builds trust with clients, directors, and audiences alike.

Consistency is a mark of professionalism. When your voice can deliver consistently, not just occasionally, you become someone others can rely on.

Endurance rep: Record 20 seconds, does your last line sound like your first?

Today invites you to slow down and build a strong foundation. Precision improves when effort softens. Clarity gets clearer when tension releases. Endurance increases when you practice patiently instead of forcing. Your goal isn't speed or perfection, but sustainable control. Relax. Even Olympians stretch before competition. Take a full, slow yawn. You have my permission.

Train Today

Return to Day 4's tongue twister list. This time, your goal is stamina, not speed. Record your reading and observe any differences between readings, especially the first and the last. Is there energy or a lack of energy in your readings?

RESToday Reflection

When does my clarity begin to decline while listening to the Day 5 Tongue Twisters Articulation Challenge recording, and how can I train to keep steady beyond that point?

DAY 6
CREATIVE REST: VOICE

*Restoring connection to your voice through
gentleness, curiosity, and release.*

In performance-driven careers, rest is often misunderstood. Many voice professionals feel pressure to stay productive, believing that continuous output equals dedication. But athletes understand a truth that artists sometimes forget, growth doesn't occur during nonstop exertion. It happens during recovery. Without rest, muscles become fatigued, coordination declines, and motivation decreases. The voice is no different.

Creative rest: Hum your favorite melody for 30 seconds, no judging.

Today is not about drills, precision, or improvement metrics. It is about a relationship. Creative rest lets you reconnect with your voice as more than just a tool for delivery. It encourages you to experience sound without judgment, expectation, or outcome. When pressure releases, the nervous system softens. Breath deepens. The voice returns to its natural rhythm.

When creativity is forced, it contracts. When it is welcomed, it opens up. Taking time to hum, speak softly, doodle, write freely, or simply listen reminds you that your voice is expressive before it is performative. This reconnection safeguards long-term joy, and joy is a vital ingredient in sustainable careers.

The Voice Athlete knows that rest is not wasted time. It is purposeful training for resilience. Creative rest helps prevent burnout, reconnects you emotionally to the work, and prepares you to come back with clarity and enthusiasm. Without it, even the most disciplined routines can feel heavy over time.

Today's work is subtle but impactful. By creating space, you build vocal reliability. You allow your voice to heal, not just physically but creatively too. Doodle break = brain recharge.

Train Today

Participate in a gentle, creative activity using your voice today without setting any goals or judging your performance.

RESToday Reflection

How does my voice feel when I let go of the pressure to perform or improve?

DAY 1
CREATIVE REST: HEALTH

Honoring the body that holds your voice.

Your voice doesn't exist on its own. It resides within your body, supported by breath, posture, hydration, sleep, nutrition, and emotional balance. Every word you speak is carried by muscles, air, and energy systems working in harmony. When the body is tired, tense, or depleted, the voice notices immediately. Tone dulls. Breath shortens. Fatigue comes on faster. What seems like a 'vocal issue' is often a full-body signal asking for care.

In performance fields, it's easy to concentrate only on technique. We rehearse scripts, refine readings, and perfect delivery while ignoring the foundation that supports those skills. But no amount of vocal training can replace chronic exhaustion or neglect. Persistent hoarseness or pain should be evaluated by an Ear, Nose, and Throat (ENT) specialist. The strongest voices are supported by strong bodies. And you only have one.

Today invites you to expand your awareness. Observe how you feel physically. How well did you sleep? Have you been consistently hydrated? Is your neck tense or are your shoulders raised? These subtle tensions build quietly, influencing how you sound before you even step into a booth. Health is not separate from artistry, it is the foundation on which artistry rests.

The Voice Athlete treats their body with respect and responsibility. Care is not a sign of weakness or indulgence, it is professionalism. By protecting your health, you safeguard your longevity. And longevity isn't just about performing well today, but about performing well for many years to come.

Body scan: Where are you tense? Pick ONE spot and soften it.

Your body isn't an obstacle to conquer, it's your greatest ally. When you nurture it, your voice gains strength, clarity, and flow. Rest is training. Period.

Train Today

Choose one restorative action today, hydrate thoroughly, stretch gently, walk, or rest silently, and consider it essential health practice.

RESToday Reflection

What does my body need most right now to support my voice in the long term?

____

____

____

____

DAY 8
CARE AS A DAILY DISCIPLINE

Small daily habits build lasting strength.

When we think about improvement, we often picture dramatic changes, longer practice sessions, bigger goals, or bursts of intense effort. But sustainable performance rarely comes from extremes. It stems from consistency. The quiet, everyday choices you make before you ever step up to the microphone have more influence on your success than any single 'big' moment.

The Voice Athlete understands that discipline isn't about pushing yourself harder. It's about showing up consistently. Drinking water before speaking, warming up gently, stretching the neck and shoulders, taking planned breaks, and prioritizing sleep, these habits may seem small or even routine, but they protect your voice more effectively than any last-minute fix. Over time, they build strength and stability.

Care streak: Choose 1 habit, do it daily for 7 days. What's your fave?

Discipline is often misunderstood as strict or harsh. In reality, it is an act of care. It involves choosing what supports you, even when it would be easier not to. It means honoring preparation when no one is watching. When care becomes routine rather than optional, performance becomes reliable rather than unpredictable. You no longer depend on luck or 'good days.' You create the conditions for success every day.

Professionalism resides in these quiet choices. The artists who endure the longest aren't usually the ones who work the hardest in short bursts, they're the ones who consistently protect their energy. Daily discipline transforms maintenance into mastery.

Today isn't about doing more, it's about doing the small things well. Posture check. Shoulders down, Superstar.

Train Today

Complete today's care checklist slowly and with focus, treating each step as vital training.

- ☐ Start the day with water, then meditation and exercise
- ☐ Continue with more water
- ☐ Do gentle warm-ups before using your voice
- ☐ Avoid unnecessary throat clearing
- ☐ Keep track of vocal fatigue throughout the day
- ☐ Maintain good posture and proper breath support
- ☐ Take vocal breaks between sessions
- ☐ Stretch your neck, shoulders, and jaw daily
- ☐ Prioritize sleep as part of your vocal recovery
- ☐ End the day with light cooldown exercises

RESToday Reflection

Which daily habit, if practiced consistently, would best improve my voice and longevity?

DAY 9
RECORDING READINESS AND MENTAL CLARITY

*Preparation keeps you calm, and being calm
boosts confident performance.*

Long before you say your first word, your environment has already influenced your performance. A cluttered desk, tangled cables, background noise, low batteries, and last-minute troubleshooting, these small distractions quietly drain your focus and energy. By the time you start recording or speaking, part of your attention has already been spent managing stress.

**Booth reset: Clear ONE thing
from your space. Less clutter,
more clarity. Invite calm in.**

The Voice Athlete knows that preparation isn't just about technique, it's mental. When your space is organized, your equipment is tested, and your materials are ready, your nervous system relaxes. That feeling of readiness sends a strong message to your body, you are safe, prepared, and capable. Breathing deepens. Shoulders relax. Your voice flows more naturally.

A peaceful environment helps you focus on storytelling and building connections instead of problem-solving. Instead of reacting to interruptions, you stay present.

Instead of rushing, you proceed with purpose. This clarity boosts not only sound quality but also confidence and endurance.

Recording readiness isn't about being perfect, it's about eliminating unnecessary friction. Small actions, like setting levels early, silencing notifications, organizing scripts, and keeping water nearby, create a solid base for smooth recording. These habits help lessen stress before it even starts.

Professionals don't wait for chaos to teach them readiness. They build it in advance. Protect your focus.

Train Today

Before your next session, prepare your space thoroughly. Test all equipment. Eliminate any distractions you can control.

- [ ] Quiet, controlled recording environment
- [ ] Consistent microphone placement
- [ ] Test levels before each session
- [ ] Silence phones and notifications
- [ ] Keep hydration nearby
- [ ] Ensure a stable internet connection
- [ ] Wear noise-free clothing and minimize movement
- [ ] Have backup power or batteries ready
- [ ] Keep session notes and scripts organized
- [ ] Maintain a clean, distraction-free mindset

RESToday Reflection

How does my environment affect my focus, energy, and
confidence when I start working?

____

____

____

____

____

____

____

____

____

____

DAY 10
WARMING UP AND COOLING DOWN

How you start and finish determines how long you last.

Athletes never sprint without warming up, but voice professionals often start demanding work with little preparation. Cold muscles, dry vocal folds, and shallow breathing increase the risk of strain, fatigue, and inconsistent sound. A proper warm-up gently activates coordination between breath, body, and voice, preparing you for the work ahead.

Warming up isn't about forcing sound, it's about gently easing the voice into motion. Gentle humming, lip trills, breath work, and light articulation exercises promote blood flow, flexibility, and resonance without strain. These small rituals signal to your nervous system that it's time to focus, helping you transition smoothly into performance mode.

**Warm-up wins: Lip trill
for 10 seconds, then smile
(yes, it changes sound).**

Cooling down is equally important, and far too often overlooked. After a long session, tension remains in the neck, jaw, shoulders, and breath. Without release, that tension persists into the rest of the day and even into tomorrow's work. A cooldown helps the voice settle, the body relax, and recovery start right away.

The Voice Athlete considers both warm-ups and cooldowns essential bookends to performance. They show respect for the voice and help ensure longevity. Starting gently and ending deliberately can reduce strain, increase consistency, and safeguard your ability to perform again. Breathe in calm. Exhale tension.

Train Today

Commit to doing a warm-up before speaking and a cooldown after every session today.

Vocal warm-up:

- Lip trills to promote airflow and relaxation
- Pitch slides to enhance flexibility and pitch range
- Gentle humming for vocal balance
- Diaphragmatic inhale/exhale cycles
- Soft cooldown hums after the session

Physical warm-up:

- Neck stretches to loosen tension
- Push-ups against your wall
- Leg lifts from your chair
- Shoulder rolls for upper-body mobility
- Jaw loosening exercises

RESToday Reflection

How does my voice feel when I take time to prepare and release rather than rush in and out of work?

____

____

____

____

____

____

____

____

____

____

DAY 11
MINDSET AND STILLNESS

Calming the mind to steady the voice.

Before the voice speaks, the mind has already set the tone. Thoughts influence breathing. Breathing shapes sound. When the mind is hurried, anxious, or distracted, the body reacts with tension, shoulders rise, breathing shortens, and the throat tightens. What often appears to be a vocal problem may be a nervous system response to mental overload.

Stillness is not passive; it is a form of training. Meditation, quiet reflection, and measured breathing help regulate the nervous system and restore balance in the body. When the mind slows, the breath deepens. When the breath deepens, the voice becomes steadier. Focus comes naturally rather than through force. These practices prepare you to face pressure with presence instead of panic.

The Voice Athlete understands that mindset isn't something you simply hope for when nerves hit. It is something you work on every day, long before the microphone is turned on. By consistently practicing stillness, you become familiar with calmness. When pressure arises, your body recognizes it and naturally returns to that state.

Spending ten to twenty minutes in quiet before vocal work isn't just a luxury, it's a performance advantage. It fosters clarity, reduces reactivity, and sharpens focus. Over time, this routine builds trust in yourself and your voice.

Stillness minute: **60 seconds of quiet breathing, start now.**

Today encourages you to pause, breathe, and listen inward. Stillness enhances performance more than force ever could.

Train Today

Spend 10–20 minutes today in meditation, or quiet breathing before vocal work with the prompts below.

- Begin sessions with gratitude and peace
- Meditate for clarity and calm
- Release performance anxiety through breath
- Focus on presence, not perfection
- Silence distractions before vocal work
- Trust preparation over outcomes
- Invite peace into your creative process
- Give yourself permission to rest
- Treat your voice as a sacred stewardship
- End the day with reflection and release

RESToday Reflection

How does my voice sound when my mind feels calm, focused, and grounded?

____

____

DAY 12
KNOWING WHEN TO STOP

Listening early promotes longevity.

In performance-driven fields, there's often an unspoken belief that pushing through discomfort shows dedication. We tell ourselves that one more take, one more read, or one more hour won't make a difference. But for voice professionals, this mindset can quietly lead to strain, fatigue, and long-term damage.

Stop sign: If your voice feels "off," what's your go-to recovery move?

Your body is always communicating. Subtle dryness, raspiness, tightness, loss of range, or extra effort to produce sound are not just inconveniences, they are signals. They serve as early warnings that your voice needs support. Ignoring these signs won't make them go away, it only delays recovery and increases the risk of more serious issues. What might have required a short break can turn into days or weeks of healing if pushed too far.

The Voice Athlete approaches limits with wisdom rather than ego. Strength does not always involve pushing forward. Sometimes, true strength is about knowing when to stop. Choosing rest early demonstrates professionalism and stewardship. It safeguards the voice that enables your work.

Learning when to stop depends on trusting that pausing now helps you perform better tomorrow. Longevity isn't about pushing every last bit of effort today but about respecting the body's need for recovery.

Today is about listening carefully and responding with kindness. Silence can be just as effective as sound.

Train Today

At the first sign of strain or fatigue today, stop and deliberately rest your voice. Persistent pain? You may need to see your Ear, Nose, and Throat (ENT) doctor.

- Sore throat, raspiness, or hoarseness
- Vocal fatigue that worsens with use
- Tightness or pain when speaking
- Loss of range or control
- Frequent throat clearing
- Burning or irritation
- Difficulty sustaining sound
- Voice cracking unexpectedly
- Persistent dryness or discomfort
- Stopping early helps maintain long-term performance

RESToday Reflection

What signals does my voice send when it needs a break, and how quickly do I respond?

DAY 13
TOOLS SUPPORTING VOICE ATHLETES

Intentionally prepare yourself to protect your voice.

Preparation is more than just a mindset, it creates an environment. Just as a professional athlete depends on the right equipment to perform well, a Voice Athlete benefits from tools that lessen strain and promote consistency. Although your voice is biological and internal, the conditions around it are incredibly important.

Dry air, dust, dehydration, and tension often go unnoticed, they build up quietly over time. Using a personal humidifier helps keep moisture levels healthy when indoor air is dry. A specially designed straw can be used for gentle semi-occluded vocal exercises that reduce pressure on the vocal folds. Saline spray and a handheld humidifier aid in nasal hydration, improving breathing efficiency and making resonance more comfortable. Even a clean, organized recording space helps minimize subtle respiratory irritation and mental distraction. Though these adjustments may seem minor, together they have a significant impact.

The Voice Athlete knows that performance is easier when friction is minimized. When your space is organized and your tools are prepared, you save energy. You concentrate on expression rather than troubleshooting. You respond instead of reacting. Equipment doesn't replace skill, it improves sustainability.

*Tool time: **Gather your tools with gratitude, for the work you get to do.***

Preparation isn't about perfection or overdoing it. It's about having a clear mindset. The right tools foster consistency, and consistency builds trust in your voice and in yourself. Pack like a pro.

Today is about preparing yourself for ease.

Train Today

Check your recording setup and voice tools today. Find one change or improvement that could lessen strain.

A few suggestions:

- A personal humidifier helps keep moisture in dry environments

- Silicone and metal straws are effective for straw phonation exercises that reduce vocal strain

- Saline spray maintains clear and hydrated nasal passages

- A noise-free hydration bottle promotes consistent water intake, not a crinkly plastic bottle. A metal or glass bottle with a wide opening is ideal

- A clean recording environment removes dust and improves air quality, which directly impacts vocal health

RESToday Reflection

What environmental or physical supports can help make my voice feel more comfortable and reliable each day?

DAY 14
THINKING LIKE A WELL-ROUNDED ARTIST

*Expanding beyond the microphone
enhances your voice within it.*

A sustainable voice career is rarely based solely on vocal ability. While technique and tone are vital, long-term resilience comes from cultivating the whole artist, not just the voice. Acting sharpens emotional authenticity. Singing improves breath control and pitch awareness. Writing enhances storytelling instincts. Coaching clarifies communication. Business literacy fosters stability and confidence in managing opportunities.

The Voice Athlete knows that developing related skills boosts performance behind the mic. When you study acting, your readings become more subtle. When you practice singing, your breath stays steadier. When you learn the business side of your craft, uncertainty drops and confidence rises. These broader abilities ease pressure on any single skill and build a stronger foundation for success.

Versatility builds resilience. When one opportunity slows down, another may emerge. When one style feels difficult, another enhances your adaptability. Creating multiple streams of creative and professional income also supports emotional stability and enriches your sense of identity beyond a single career path. It also helps you manage your energy more effectively and avoid overusing your voice just to stay stable. When your livelihood isn't reliant on saying yes to everything, you gain the freedom to protect your voice and how you use it.

Skill stack: Pick 1: acting / singing / writing / biz, what are you training today?

It's okay if your life has more than one path. You can be an athlete and star in a film, play an instrument at concerts, own a business, and still be fully dedicated in each area. Multiple streams of income don't mean you're unfocused. Multiple streams of income are important. Sometimes provision comes through more than one door, and that's not a distraction, it's wisdom. You are allowed to build stability, make an impact, and honor your calling in more than one way. Be the star of your craft at any age. Knowledge is key. Train smart. Stay ready.

Thinking like a well-rounded voice doesn't mean doing everything at once. It means staying curious, growing deliberately, and understanding that your voice exists within a larger creative ecosystem. The more complete your development, the more stable your performance becomes.

Today encourages you to look past the microphone and invest in a wider version of yourself.

Train Today

Select one complementary skill to focus on this week, acting, singing, writing, coaching, entrepreneurial literacy, or business development.

RESToday Reflection

What area of growth beyond my immediate vocal work could most strengthen my long-term career?

DAY 15
NUTRITION, TIMING, AND VOCAL SUPPORT

Fuel your body wisely so your voice can perform dependably.

Your voice might feel like an artistic tool, but it is powered by biology. Every sound you make relies on breath support, muscle coordination, hydration, and energy, factors influenced by what and when you eat. Nutrition is often overlooked in voice work, yet it directly impacts stamina, clarity, and comfort. What you eat today can either support your performance or work against it quietly.

Certain foods and habits cause unnecessary issues. Carbonation can introduce extra air, leading to discomfort. Fried or greasy foods may increase inflammation or reflux. Eating too late or too heavily before sessions can cause sluggishness or throat irritation. Alcohol and dehydration dry out tissues that need moisture to function properly. Even small choices like drinking ice-cold water, eating dairy, or speaking nonstop without breaks can affect how your voice feels.

The Voice Athlete approaches nutrition with awareness rather than restriction. The aim is not perfection but support. Balanced meals, consistent hydration, and thoughtful timing build a stable foundation for vocal work. Anti-inflammatory foods, proper rest after eating, working, and exercising, along with regular water intake, help maintain flexibility and ease. When your body feels steady, your voice responds reliably.

Fuel swap: **Choose a voice-friendly snack today.**

Professional performance starts long before the microphone is turned on. Fueling your body wisely means caring for your voice from the inside out. Instead of reacting to discomfort later, prevent it with small, purposeful choices throughout the day. Snack smart. Your voice thanks you.

Today is about refining your habits so your voice can perform at its best.

Train Today

Make one conscious nutrition choice today that promotes hydration, energy, and vocal comfort.

Do:

- Eat balanced meals
- Stay well-hydrated
- Plan your meals carefully
- Select anti-inflammatory foods
- Rest after eating

Avoid:

- Carbonated drinks before sessions
- Ffried or greasy foods

- Overeating late at night
- Alcohol before vocal work
- Cold drinking water

RESToday Reflection

How do my current eating and drinking habits influence
how my voice feels during sessions?

____

____

____

____

____

____

____

____

____

DAY 16
MINDSHIFTS FOR LONGEVITY

---

*Train your mindset to support the
career you want to maintain.*

Many challenges in voice performance are mental rather than technical. The beliefs you hold about productivity, success, and worth quietly influence how you treat your body and voice. If you think that rest is laziness or that saying yes to everything shows commitment, you might constantly overextend yourself. Over time, this mindset leads not to growth but to burnout.

The Voice Athlete understands that longevity starts with thought patterns. Building sustainable careers relies not just on intensity, but on consistency and self-respect. When you shift your mindset from 'How much can I push?' to 'How well can I sustain?,' everything shifts. Rest becomes a strategic choice. Preparation becomes empowering. Care transforms into a discipline rather than indulgence.

Mindset training is just as vital as vocal training. You constantly talk to yourself through expectations, judgments, and internal pressure. Learning to replace harsh self-talk with supportive, realistic thinking helps your nervous system relax and improves your performance. Confidence builds when your inner dialogue becomes steady instead of critical.

Mindset flip: Replace "I have to" with "I get to." Say it out loud.

Your body is the vessel for your voice. When you treat it with respect and patience, your work becomes more sustainable and enjoyable. Longevity isn't achieved through heroic effort, it's built through daily, mindful choices.

Today encourages you to become aware of your beliefs and softly modify the ones that no longer help you. Small mental shifts lead to lasting change.

Train Today

Choose one mindset shift today, and practice it with silence and focus.

- ☐ The body is a vocal carrier
- ☐ Rest as a part of training
- ☐ Consistency outweighs intensity
- ☐ Preparation eases anxiety
- ☐ Recovery safeguards longevity
- ☐ Discipline fosters freedom
- ☐ Care is not weakness
- ☐ Focus is trainable
- ☐ Sustainability equals success
- ☐ Stewardship amplifies impact

RESToday Reflection

What belief about work or success might be leading to unnecessary pressure or exhaustion?

DAY 17
THE WEEKLY RESET

Reflection fosters clarity, and clarity leads to improvement.

Progress isn't just built through action but also through awareness. In fast-paced creative careers, it's easy to keep moving forward without taking time to evaluate what's truly working. You finish one session, move on to the next, and then the next, until days start to blur. Without reflection, effort can feel endless yet aimless.

Weekly reset: What worked this week? What's getting benched?

Athletes regularly review their performance by watching footage, assessing technique, and adjusting their training plans. They understand that more work doesn't automatically lead to better results. Instead, they step back to learn. The Voice Athlete adopts the same habit. A weekly reset allows you to honestly evaluate your routines, energy, and outcomes without judgment.

Reflection helps you recognize patterns. Perhaps certain times of day feel more powerful. Maybe specific habits protect your voice while others quietly weaken it. You might find that rest enhances quality more than extra hours of practice. These insights are valuable because they enable you to train smarter instead of simply training harder.

A reset isn't about criticism; it's about course correction. It allows you to let go of what doesn't serve you and strengthen what does. As awareness grows, effort becomes more deliberate, and growth more effective. Mindset flex: You're stronger today.

Today is your chance to pause, breathe, and reset. Progress speeds up when you understand yourself clearly.

Train Today

Set aside some quiet time today to review your week and identify one adjustment that will help you move forward.

RESToday Reflection

What habits boosted my performance this week, and what might I kindly adjust next week?

____

____

____

____

____

____

DAY 18
BREATH AS THE FOUNDATION

Strong breath produces a strong sound.

Before tone, before articulation, before expression, there is breath. Every word you speak rests on air. Breath is the quiet engine that powers your voice, yet it is often the most overlooked part of vocal training. Many voice professionals focus on what they hear while forgetting the invisible force that makes sound possible.

When breath is shallow or rushed, the body compensates by lifting the shoulders, tightening the throat, and working the jaw harder. Strain appears where there should be ease. Fatigue sets in more quickly because the voice is being pushed instead of supported. What feels like a vocal issue is often actually a breathing problem.

The Voice Athlete knows that breath is not automatic, it is trainable. Diaphragmatic breathing enhances control, boosts stamina, and shields the vocal folds from unnecessary pressure. When breath flows steadily, sound flows naturally. Projection requires less effort. Phrases feel supported rather than forced. Confidence grows as your body feels grounded and stable.

Breath also influences your mindset. Slow, deliberate breathing calms the nervous system and eases anxiety. It centers you before auditions and keeps you steady during long sessions. In this way, breath is both a physical support and an emotional regulator, the link between body and mind. Progress trumps perfection every time.

Breath drill: In 4… hold 2… out 6… repeat x 3. Game changer!

Training your breath is like strengthening your foundation. When the base is solid, everything built on top becomes simpler. Today is about returning to that base and honoring the most straightforward, yet powerful tool you have. Breath is free insurance for performance.

Train Today

Practice slow diaphragmatic breathing for five to ten minutes today, focusing on relaxed, steady airflow. Refer to day #11 if you run out of breathing ideas.

RESToday Reflection

How does my voice change when my breath feels deep, calm, and supported?

____

____

____

____

DAY 19
ENERGY MANAGEMENT

Guard your energy as purposefully as you guard your voice.

Time management is important, but energy management is crucial. You may have plenty of hours in your day but still struggle to perform if your energy is low. Voice work requires mental focus, emotional engagement, and physical endurance. Without enough energy, even simple tasks become difficult and draining.

Many voice professionals underestimate how much energy storytelling requires. Every read demands attention, interpretation, breath control, and emotional engagement. If you move from one session to another without pause, your body and mind begin to lag behind your expectations. Fatigue often shows up first, voice tension creeps in, clarity softens, and patience shortens.

*Energy break: **Energy low?
Get up. Stretch. Air punch.
x 10. You're welcome.***

The Voice Athlete manages energy carefully. This involves scheduling demanding work during peak focus hours, taking breaks between sessions, setting your watch or phone, and recognizing when rest improves quality more than pushing forward. Energy is not unlimited, it must be replenished through sleep, hydration, movement, and quiet moments of reset. Protecting energy is not about doing less, it is about doing better.

When you manage your energy intentionally, your performance becomes more consistent. You avoid the extremes of burnout and overextension. You become steady instead of reactive. Over time, this steadiness builds resilience and longevity.

Today encourages you to notice not just your busyness but also how energized you feel. Sustainable performance relies on both.

Train Today

Schedule at least one purposeful break today to refresh your mind and body before continuing your work.

- [ ] Get out of that chair and stretch for 15 minutes
- [ ] Stand up and do push-ups against the wall or desk
- [ ] Take a deep breath and scream out loud
- [ ] Do 10 minutes of chair strengthening with resistance bands
- [ ] Look around your space and write down 10 things you are grateful for
- [ ] Are you throwing air punches?
- [ ] Energy is low—walk it out

RESToday Reflection

When do I feel most energized and focused, and how can I organize my work around those times?

DAY 20
BOUNDARIES THAT SAFEGUARD THE VOICE

---

*Setting boundaries that safeguard your
energy, time, and long-term well-being.*

In creative careers, opportunities can feel urgent and endless. Another audition. Another session. Another favor. Another 'quick' project. Saying yes often becomes automatic, driven by fear of missing out or the belief that more work always leads to more success. But without boundaries, even meaningful work can become overwhelming, and eventually, that overwhelm shows up in the voice.

Your voice cannot detach itself from your schedule. When you push your time and energy too far, recovery vanishes. Fatigue grows. Focus diminishes. Tension rises. The outcome isn't better performance, but decreased performance. The Voice Athlete understands that limits are not restrictions, they are protections. Boundaries create space to prepare, recover, and show up fully where it matters most.

Saying no can sometimes be the most professional choice. It helps you honor your existing commitments and maintain quality instead of rushing through everything at half effort. Boundaries show self-respect, and self-respect supports longevity. When you protect your time, you protect your abilities. When you give only half effort, they notice it, and they hear it.

Establishing boundaries may feel uncomfortable at first, especially if you're used to pleasing others or constantly pushing yourself. But over time, they bring clarity and confidence. You stop reacting to every demand and start responding with intention. And you sleep so much better at night. No is vocal protection.

*Boundary move: **No is a complete sentence.***

Today is about prioritizing sustainability over urgency. You don't have to do everything to succeed. You only need to focus on what truly matters and do it well.

Train Today

Identify one area where you can establish a healthy boundary today. Is it saying no to a request? Scheduling recovery time? Or limiting overwork? Maybe no electronics, just silence?

RESToday Reflection

Where in my schedule do I need to set stronger boundaries to protect my energy and voice?

____

____

____

DAY 21
AUDITIONS AS ATHLETIC TRAINING

Every opportunity is a rep that builds your skill and resilience.

Auditions can carry emotional weight. It's easy to see each one as a test of worth, a pass or fail moment that determines your value as a voice professional. When viewed this way, auditions feel heavy, stressful, and personal. Nerves rise. Pressure builds. You start to crave callbacks. The experience becomes something to survive rather than something to learn from.

But athletes perceive repetition differently. Every practice rep, drill, and scrimmage is simply training. It isn't proof of success or failure, it's preparation. The Voice Athlete benefits from adopting this same mindset. An audition isn't a verdict. It's a rep, an opportunity to refine technique, explore choices, and build adaptability.

When you approach auditions as a chance to practice instead of a test, your body relaxes. Breath flows more easily. Performance feels more natural and less forced. You stop chasing perfection and start focusing on being present. You begin to inhabit the character rather than perform it. Ironically, this relaxed confidence often leads to better results. You sound more authentic because you're not trying to 'win,' you're simply performing. Just bring yourself.

Each opportunity gains you experience. Every script refines your instincts. Every submission boosts your efficiency. Over time, these small repetitions lead to mastery. What once felt intimidating becomes second nature. Confidence increases because you've prepared for it. What once took hours now only takes minutes.

***

*Audition rep: **Do one cold read, no redo. What did you learn?***

***

Today encourages you to change your perspective. You're not here to prove yourself, you're honing your craft. The result is less important than the growth. Auditions = practice. You're training. Remember, train smart, stay ready.

Train Today

Treat your next audition or practice read like a training session. Prioritize learning over self-criticism.

RESToday Reflection

How would my performance improve if I saw every opportunity as practice rather than pressure?

____

____

____

DAY 22
PRESENCE OVER PERFECTION

Connection matters more than anything, flawlessness.

Many voice professionals quietly pursue perfection. You rehearse lines repeatedly, analyze every syllable, and try to eliminate every possible mistake. While preparation is important, perfectionism often creates tension instead of excellence. The more you try to control every detail, the more rigid your voice can become. Breath shortens. Delivery stiffens. Authenticity fades.

Presence beats perfect: Deliver one line like you're talking to ONE person you love.

Audiences and listeners rarely connect with perfection, they connect with presence. They respond to sincerity, emotion, and truth. A technically flawless read without heart can feel distant, while a somewhat imperfect read filled with genuine connection can feel unforgettable. The Voice Athlete understands that the goal is not mechanical precision, but meaningful communication.

Presence requires relaxation and trust. It involves letting go of constant self-monitoring and fully inhabiting the message. When you stop worrying about how you sound and focus on what you're saying, your voice naturally becomes warmer and more expressive. Confidence grows because you're no longer trying to perform perfectly, you're simply being present.

Perfectionism often whispers that you're not ready yet. Presence reminds you that you already are. When you show up fully, listeners feel it immediately. Your voice carries intention rather than tension.

Today is an invitation to let go of the pressure to be perfect and instead focus on connection. Your humanity is what makes your voice powerful. Connection always beats perfection.

Train Today

Next time you read, concentrate on meaning and connection instead of technical perfection.

RESToday Reflection

When do I feel most present and authentic while speaking, and what helps me access that state?

____

____

____

____

DAY 23
VOCAL VARIETY AND FLEXIBILITY

A flexible voice is a strong voice.

Repetition is a natural part of professional voice work. You might spend hours reading in similar tones, pitches, and pacing patterns. While consistency has value, remaining stuck in one vocal register or delivery style for too long can quietly cause tension and fatigue. Just like any muscle group, the voice needs variety and movement. When you ask the same muscles to perform the same way constantly, they tire more quickly.

Vocal variety is not only an artistic skill but also a physical one. Show some range. Shifting pitch, pace, resonance, and emotional tone distributes effort across different muscle groups and reduces strain. These subtle changes protect stamina and keep the voice feeling responsive rather than stuck. A flexible voice moves easily between styles, emotions, and demands without forcing or overworking.

The Voice Athlete views flexibility as both a form of expression and a form of protection. Exploring different textures, rhythms, and dynamics broadens your range as a storyteller while supporting longevity. Variety keeps the voice lively and adaptable. It enables you to respond natu-rally to scripts instead of forcing a single habitual sound.

When you loosen your approach, creativity grows. You find new colors and options in your delivery. Sessions feel less dull and more lively. Your voice stays fresher because it isn't limited to one narrow path.

*Flex play: **Read the same line 3 ways: calm / hype / direct.***

Today is about giving your voice space to flow. Flexibility boosts resilience, and resilience supports careers.

Train Today

Try out different pitch, pace, and tone during today's practice. Experiment with at least three different delivery styles for the same script. Go over the top if there's room.

RESToday Reflection

Where do I tend to rely on the same vocal habits, and how could adding more variety enhance both my sound and stamina?

____

____

____

____

____

DAY 24
THE ROLE OF ENVIRONMENT

*Your physical space influences your sound
more than you might think.*

It's easy to think of vocal performance as something that solely happens within the body, breath, technique, articulation, and mindset. However, your environment plays an equally important role. The air you breathe, your posture, the noise you block out, and the space you work in all affect how your voice feels and functions. Your surroundings aren't separate from your performance, they are part of it.

Environment tweak: Bless your environment. Create a space of peace.

Dry air can irritate the throat and limit vocal flexibility. Dust or poor air quality can hinder breathing and resonance. Harsh lighting or uncomfortable seating causes subtle tension in the neck and shoulders. Even background noise or visual clutter can distract you and increase mental fatigue. These factors may seem small individually, but together they influence how easily your voice flows.

The Voice Athlete considers their environment a silent teammate. Instead of adapting to uncomfortable conditions, you modify the space to support your body. A humidifier, clean air, good posture, soft lighting, and organized materials. These small choices reduce friction and save energy. When your environment supports you, you need less effort to perform well.

Creating a supportive space isn't about perfection or costly equipment, it's about intention. A calm, clean, and comfortable environment helps you relax into your work. Relaxation leads to better breathing, which in turn results in better sound.

Today encourages you to observe what your space communicates. Your voice needs an environment that allows it to flourish. Clean space. Clear voice. Calm mind.

Train Today

Improve one aspect of your workspace today, adjust air quality, posture, lighting, or organization.

RESToday Reflection

How does my current environment support or impede my vocal comfort and focus?

____

____

____

____

DAY 25

RESPONDING TO FATIGUE WITH COMPASSION

View fatigue as a message, not a setback.

In high-performance settings, fatigue is often misunderstood. Many professionals see tiredness as weakness or a lack of discipline, something to push through instead of recognizing. You might tell yourself to 'just power through' or 'finish one more take.' However, this mindset can cause more harm than progress over time. Fatigue is not a flaw, it serves as communication.

Your body constantly sends signals. A heavy voice, reduced clarity, slower recall, or difficulty sustaining breath are not inconveniences, they are messages. They tell you that energy reserves are low and recovery is needed. Ignoring these signals does not build strength. It builds strain. And strain quietly accumulates until performance suffers.

The Voice Athlete faces fatigue with curiosity instead of criticism. Instead of forcing productivity, you pause to evaluate. Do you need water? Movement? Silence? Rest? Often, small acts of care restore clarity faster than pushing through ever could. Compassion becomes a strategic advantage. When you respond early, recovery is quicker, and your performance stays steady.

This approach isn't about doing less, it's about doing what's sustainable. By respecting your limits, you safeguard your long-term health. You make sure that today's effort doesn't deplete tomorrow's capacity.

*Compassion check: **Tired? Water + 2 minutes silence. Then decide.***

Strength isn't measured by how long you ignore fatigue, it's measured by how wisely you respond to it. Fatigue whispers. Listen early.

Today, encourage yourself to listen more carefully and be patient. Your voice will thank you for it.

Train Today

At the first sign of fatigue today, take a brief restorative break instead of pushing yourself further.

RESToday Reflection

How do I usually react when I'm tired, and what would happen if I responded with compassion instead of pressure?

DAY 26
CONFIDENCE GROWS THROUGH PREPARATION

Preparation transforms nervousness into confidence.

Confidence is often mistaken for personality. Some people seem naturally calm under pressure, while others feel nervous before every session or audition. However, confidence is not something you are born with, it is something you develop. The foundation of that confidence is preparation.

When you walk into a recording session unprepared, your mind races to catch up. You question your choices. You second-guess your delivery. Breathing becomes shallow. Tension grows. What you call 'nerves' is often just uncertainty. The body responds to the unknown by tightening up. The voice follows.

Prep power: **Prepared beats panicked. Every time.**

The Voice Athlete knows that preparation makes a difference. When you warm up your voice, review your script, set up your space, and take care of your body, you build stability. Your nervous system eases because you're confident you've done the work. You stop hoping things will go well and start trusting that they will. Preparation replaces panic with focus.

Confidence, then, is not bravado, it is familiarity. It is the quiet assurance that comes from repetition and preparation. Each small act of readiness becomes a vote of trust in yourself. Over time, those votes accumulate. What once felt intimidating begins to feel manageable, even routine. Prepared beats panicked. Every time.

Today is about leaning into readiness. Instead of trying to force confidence in the moment, build it beforehand. When preparation is consistent, confidence comes naturally.

Train Today

Prepare one step earlier than usual today, warm up longer, review your script more thoroughly, or organize your space ahead of time.

RESToday Reflection

How does my confidence differ when I feel fully prepared compared to when I feel rushed or uncertain?

DAY 27
RECOVERY AS A COMPETITIVE EDGE

Rest strategically to perform well consistently.

In a culture that often celebrates constant hustle, rest can feel unnatural. It might seem like slowing down means falling behind. But in high-performance fields, both athletic and creative, the opposite is true. Recovery is not time wasted. It's where strength gets rebuilt. Without it, even the most talented voice professionals eventually run out of energy.

When you work nonstop without rest, exhaustion builds up. Muscles tighten. Focus diminishes. The voice loses flexibility and resilience. You might find yourself pushing harder just to keep the same results. This isn't progress, it's depletion. The Voice Athlete understands that sustainable performance depends on cycles of effort and recovery working together.

Recovery is proactive, not accidental. It involves planning rest, hydration, stretching, sleep, and quiet time as intentionally as you schedule sessions, movie shoots, speaking engagements, or auditions. It means giving your voice space to heal before strain occurs. These practices restore both the body and mind, sharpening clarity and stamina for what's ahead. Uninterrupted sleep overnight. Naps during the day. Minutes of silence. They all move the needle.

Strategic rest becomes a competitive advantage because it helps you stay consistent. While others burn out or fluctuate, you remain steady. Your voice stays reliable. Your energy stays available. You show up ready, not drained.

Recovery flex: Schedule 15 minutes of "nothing." Put it on the calendar. Bravo!

Recovery is not a reward you earn after exhaustion. It is a tool you use to prevent exhaustion in the first place.

Today encourages you to see rest in a new way. When you honor recovery, you invest in longevity.

Train Today

Schedule focused recovery time today: stretch, hydrate, walk, play an instrument, or rest, and treat it as essential training.

RESToday Reflection

How does my performance vary when I give myself enough time to recover fully between periods of effort?

____

____

____

____

DAY 28
GRATITUDE AND PERSPECTIVE

Gratitude calms the heart and strengthens the soul's voice.

In competitive industries, it's easy to concentrate on what's next, the next booking, opportunity, award, stage, arena, movie, or milestone. Ambition fuels growth, but always looking forward can subtly create tension. When your mind is fixed only on what hasn't happened yet, anxiety increases, and satisfaction diminishes. The voice mirrors that internal pressure.

Gratitude reps: Write 3 wins from your voice journey, big or tiny. Just three, right?

Gratitude shifts perspective. It slows the sense of urgency and reminds you of what is already here, the ability to speak, the lives you've changed, the opportunity to create, the progress you've made, and the skills you've developed. These are not small things, they are foundations. When you pause to acknowledge them, your nervous system relaxes, breath deepens, the body softens, and your voice carries steadiness instead of striving.

The Voice Athlete knows that perspective safeguards longevity. Gratitude lessens comparison and performance anxiety. It reconnects you with purpose rather than pressure. When you remember why you started connecting, storytelling, serving, and expressing, the work becomes meaningful beyond just metrics and outcomes.

Gratitude balances ambition. It allows you to pursue growth without losing peace. Over time, this emotional stability helps maintain consistent performance and resilience through both success and setbacks. Gratitude sounds better on everyone.

Today encourages you to move from urgency to gratitude. A thankful heart creates a steady voice.

Train Today

Write down three specific things you're truly grateful for today about your voice or career.

RESToday Reflection

How does focusing on gratitude influence my work and performance approach?

____

____

____

____

____

DAY 29
INTEGRATION AND REFLECTION

Lasting growth occurs when lessons turn into habits.

Over the past few weeks, you have practiced new skills, gained awareness, and tried out healthier ways to care for your voice and body. You have warmed up daily, rested wisely, listened to your limits, and built mental resilience. But learning alone does not lead to transformation. True change happens when insights become routine.

Gathering information is easy, but integrating it is more challenging and powerful. Without reflection, even valuable lessons fade from memory. Habits revert to autopilot. The Voice Athlete understands that progress isn't just about adding new practices but about choosing which ones to carry forward consistently. True growth happens through integration, making it sustainable.

Today is a pause point, a moment to reflect on what has shifted. Maybe your voice feels steadier. Perhaps your energy is more predictable. You might find yourself warming up automatically or taking breaks without guilt. These small changes matter because they show your training is becoming instinctive, not forced.

Reflection isn't about judging what you did 'right' or 'wrong.' It's about gaining clarity. What went well? What felt supportive? What would you change? When you evaluate with curiosity rather than criticism, you make smarter choices moving forward. Revisit Day #1. You're already stronger.

*Integration pick: **List 7 habits you're keeping, circle your top 3.***

The goal is not perfection. It is alignment. Sustainable performance comes from a few well-chosen habits practiced daily. Doesn't a garden grow from a few well-watered seeds?

Train Today

Reflect on the past 28 days and select three practices you will commit to sustaining long-term.

RESToday Reflection

Which habits have had the biggest positive impact on my voice, energy, or mindset?

____

____

____

____

DAY 30
CARRYING THE VOICE ATHLETE FORWARD

This is not the finish line, it is the foundation.

Thirty days ago, you made a simple but powerful decision, to show up for your voice with intention. Not just to perform, but to train. Not just to work, but to care. Day by day, you practiced awareness, built habits, protected your energy, and redefined what it means to be a professional voice talent. What may have started as small daily actions has quietly grown into something much larger, consistency, resilience, and trust in yourself.

The Voice Athlete mindset isn't about quick fixes or fleeting motivation. It centers on sustainability. Over these past weeks, you've learned that hydration, rest, breath, mindset, and you matter. You've seen that preparation builds confidence, recovery promotes longevity, and small habits lead to big change. You've trained not only your voice but also your discipline, awareness, and self-respect.

And now, something important has shifted. Many of these practices probably feel less forced and more natural. Warm-ups might happen automatically. Breaks might feel justified rather than guilty. You may notice yourself listening more carefully to your body and responding with care instead of pressure. This is what real growth looks like, not dramatic transformation, but steady alignment.

Today is not an ending, it's a beginning. The goal was never just to finish the Voice Athlete Method and stop. It was to develop a way of thinking and working that endures beyond these pages. The Voice Athlete identity remains with you in every audition, every session, every breath. If you're ready for the challenge, repeat every 30 days. Champion status, unlocked. You did it!

Train Today

Write a brief message to your future self, explaining how you'll keep taking care of your voice after today.

RESToday Reflection

What three habits or mindset shifts will I adopt to safeguard my voice and career in the long run?

*Coach note: **Champion unlocked.***

YOUR TRAINING DOESN'T END HERE

You didn't just finish thirty days, you developed the discipline that sustains careers.

Thirty days of slowing down.
Thirty days of listening to your body.
Thirty days of strengthening your voice, mindset, and discipline.

Pause for a moment and consider what that signifies.

You didn't rush.
You didn't give up.
You didn't wait for motivation.

You showed up every day.

That's what athletes do.

And now, something subtle yet powerful has shifted.

Your awareness is sharper.
Your preparation is steadier.
Your voice feels more supported.
Your nervous system recovers faster.

You're no longer just reacting to your work, you're training for it.

But here's the truth that every top voice professional knows.

Training isn't seasonal, it's ongoing.

Care doesn't stop when the program ends.
It evolves into a rhythm.

Just like hydration.
Just like breathing, like warm-ups.

It becomes a part of how you live.

Now let's live this standard of excellence together!

THE VOICE ATHLETE MANIFESTO

Listen up.

Your voice isn't fragile.
It's powerful.
But power without training burns out the person who wields it.

Talent got you here.
Discipline will keep you here.

Hydrate.
Warm up.
Focus.
Recover.

Excellence isn't loud.
It's consistent.

And consistency wins on game day.

This is how careers last.
This is how champions sound.

Now, lace up.
Lock in.
Train like you mean it.
I'll see you there.

—Coach K. Brenai

~ Certificate of Completion ~

THE
30-DAY
VOICE ATHLETE STRATEGY

A Daily Guide with Secret Sauce
for Moving Beyond Obstacles

This certifies that

(Your Name)

has become intentional, mindful, and performance-ready!

Steady our breath and sharpen our focus as we step into the work before us. Let our love for this craft grow deeper, grounded in knowledge and guided by discernment, so we pursue what is excellent and release what is not. Strengthen our discipline in the unseen preparation, protect our voice under pressure, and guard our minds from fear and our bodies from strain. When the door opens, let us walk in prepared, when the moment comes, let us stand steady, and when the work is done, let us leave stronger than we arrived. May we train with intention, steward the gift entrusted to us, and show up ready, always giving back with gratitude for the opportunities placed in our hands. _(Your commitment to your voice and your craft)_

Completion Date: _______________ _Signature:_ _______________

For more about the RESToday app:

www.RESTodayApp.com

Visit Keaver at:

www.KeaverBrenai.com